HEAVENLY GUIDANCE
Angel Cards

BY
ANGEL INTUITIVE
AMELIA BERT

Copyright © 2018 by Amelia Bert

This book is not intended to be a substitute for the medical advice of a licensed physician. The reader should consult with their doctor in any matters relating to his/her health.

For information on special discounts for bulk purchases, please contact us via email at: amelia@ameliabert.com

Visit website at: ameliabert.com

TABLE OF CONTENTS

YOU CAN PURCHASE THE "HEAVENLY GUIDANCE ANGEL CARDS" FROM THIS LINK:

http://bit.ly/2ElTZHA

Preface

I have always been fascinated with divination cards. Since I was little I loved looking at the different images on the cards and trying to pick the ones that caught my attention. Of course it was a child's play then, I did not give any attention to spreads, and thorough meanings, yet the thought that these beautiful set of cards spoke to me and answered my questions was astonishing to me. Now, years later I still find it exciting to use them.

I have to admit, the reason for creating this card deck is half selfish. _(Cheeks turn red)_ I wanted to create a set of cards for my own use, so that I can connect with my angels on the go. The other half of the reason is because I wanted to help people connect with their own Angels for support. As an angel intuitive, I have the gift to be able to connect with my guides directly, in times of crisis, when I'm in need of guidance and support. I find this a huge help and something that I wish many of you have as well. I know how hard it is when you are in need of some support, and you don't know where to turn to. For this, I wanted these cards to be your own support and assistance, your own connection to Angels and spiritual helpers.

As an angel intuitive, I decided to work with Archangel Gabriel, who is great in delivering messages, to help me create this deck, alongside with a team of angel guides. I asked them to help create a set of cards that will help connect their guidance to the person using it. The angels directed every theme and card meaning after that. It is similar to some of the best guidance I have received from them over the years, and now you can have it too, whenever you need it.

If you are wondering about the size of the cards and how it's different from other oracle or angel cards there is a reason for it. Some people like me have smaller hands and thus, the usual 3.5x5.5 size, just can't fit the hand. For this, it makes the cards harder to shuffle. Also, I wanted you to able to hold all the cards in your hands, so you will be able to spread your energy evenly to them. Your energy is important to the cards you see. If you are not certain on how to interpret or spread them, you don't need to worry. The good thing about this card is that, it's fairly easy to use for anyone.

HEAVENLY GUIDANCE: *The Booklet*

INTRODUCTION

Angel cards are much similar to tarot cards. However, unlike the tarot cards the messages are very soothing and loving. They never bring any negative messages. Due to their high frequency and kind meanings, they attract lighted beings such as angels that bring you messages through them. In the point of this angel card deck, the Angel energy did form the meanings, which makes it even more pure and divinely connected.

If you have ever wondered if Angel cards or tarot cards work as divination tools, the answer is yes. As you focus on a question, spirits follow your thoughts that reply with the right cards. There is a process that needs to be followed for an accurate reading. The cards you pick play an important rule, but same is to trust your intuition to interpret them. Spirit directs the energy of the cards so that the appropriate card may fall off the deck, strike your attention, or even guide your movements to pick the suited ones.

For interpreting the cards, make reference to this booklet for any card you pick; however, spirit directs the interpretation of each card through intuition as well. The more skilled you become, the more you understand the meaning of the cards without even needing the booklet to help you.

You can use this Angel cards to answer your own questions, get guidance, or assist someone else by using the cards for them.

The meanings of each card is channeled directly by the angels as if they were speaking to you. Know that as you pray, their presence is with you at that time, helping you towards the right card for guidance.

HOW TO USE ANGEL CARDS:

1. Find a quiet place where you won't have any distractions. It's important that you quiet your mind before you begin. Focus on your breathing, clear away any thoughts.

2. Cleanse your cards. Your cards may hold negative energy that makes them "heavy" and confuse you when choosing the right card to read. There are several ways you can cleanse your cards.

a. Invoke Archangel Michael.

"I ask for the loving Archangel Michael, please step forth and join me now. Please cleanse my cards, and remove any negative energy so that they only bring me accurate answers to my questions. Thank you, and so it is."

b. Tap the cards twice, and imagine that any negative energy that they hold, drops and dissolves.

c. Hold the cards. In your mind ask that they are completely cleansed. Imagine white, cleansing light surrounding you and the cards.

d. Crystal cleansing. You can place a cleansing crystal on the deck for a few hours. The crystal will absorb any negative energy.

3. Invite Angels and lighted beings to help you with the reading.

> *"I call upon lighted Angels to bring me accurate answers through these cards. Please guide my hands to pick the right cards, guide my thoughts to give accurate interpretations. Guide me on what I should know. Thank you, thank you, thank you."*

4. Ask a question. As you shuffle the cards ask them a question. The more specific question, the more appropriate will be the answer. Remember, the future is yet unknown, or there are multiple possibilities, so avoid asking any questions about

the future. As these cards do not work as divination, avoid asking what will happen, instead say: what do you want me to know, or how can you guide me on this situation.

5. Choose the right cards. There are several ways you can do this.

When you ask your question and a card falls off the deck, you better choose that card as there is a reason it fell off the deck.

a. You can spread the cards in front of you and follow your gaze. You are guided towards the right card with your eyes. If a card gets your attention more than the others, pick that one.

b. You can shuffle, cut the deck in half, and pick the first cards in the order they appear.

c. You can close your eyes and follow your hands as they choose the right cards from the pile.

6. Spread your cards. There are several ways you can position the cards.

If you are familiar with one particular way of card spread, then use that one. From my experience

I did not find correlation between specific card spreads. For this I choose a simple and convenient spread. I usually choose 6 cards and place them 3x2 without paying any extra attention to their position. If you want a more indebt analysis on a topic you can always try 9 cards (3x3).

When I am confused about a card and what it represents, I pick another card from the deck and combine their messages. For instance if you picked the card "kindness" and you are confused about what it might represent, pray for another card to help you understand the guidance better. If the second card is "nurture", then the angels want to guide you to receive some assistance from your mother, or that she requires your assistance.

Another example is if you receive "Creativity" and then "sequences". The angels want to tell you to give more attention to your thoughts, an idea keeps repeating but you neglect it. It's time to put that idea into action and work on a great project.

7. Interpret the cards. You can either choose the deck's booklet to help you with the interpretations,

or you can trust your intuition about what each card means.

Remember to be open to any answers you receive.

8. When you have completed the reading, thank the Angels for assisting you.

CARDS AND DIVINATION

I know many of you are wondering whether using cards, (any cards angel or otherwise) is wrong. I have decided to ask the angels and let their words answer to you directly.

Is using divination tools such as cards, wrong? How should we use divination tools the right way so that they are acceptable by you?

If divination tools as you call them, are used to predict the future or to force guidance to appear, or asked to make choices for you, then in any way and form they are used, it is wrong.

We are aware that so many of you use divination tools with a pure heart, not meant to spread harm or act unjustly. Even those you call angel cards or those means that you pray to holy spirits to respond through, if done so to force those mentioned above, then the guidance that you seek will not come through. It is not because we don't want to help you but there are some answers that we cannot give you. Firstly questions about the future are unpredictable. As future changes, as you change, so do your choices and your future. We cannot respond to you if you ask us what will happen, simply because it is not predestined.

What's more is asking us what to do. Deciding for you is not the way that God instructs. We can help you shed some light in one way or the other, or guide you to find the right path, but we cannot make any decision for you or force you to change your mind. For this, we are very careful when helping you about such matters. When you ask us for guidance and the cards interpretation are fixed and they give you "yes do this" or "no don't act", then if we give you one or the other card we are forcing the decisions.

Another matter that is hard to define through divination tools is giving you clear guidance. Yes, we can help you through angel cards, or pendulum drawing or any other tool, but the guidance is very restricted. If you don't use your intuition to receive direct messages then the interpretation and guidance is vague and can be easily misinterpreted.

Many times, the words we want to say to you don't belong in cards and are not a yes/ no sort of answer. Instead of giving you false guidance, we don't respond. Many times your questions are full of ego and you force one answer to come through and denying anything other than that. The ego makes you see what you want. "Yes you will get a lot of money," "yes you will meet your true partner," "no you don't need to act". Many of the answers are ego based and not angel inspired. For this, you should be very careful when using any sort of divination tools as the answers might not be from source.

Also, using any sort of divination without prayer, is inventing all sort of energies to mend with your tools and guide them. In this case, the answers can be false and not true. For this, we want you to be aware of the loopholes inherent in them.

With all of these in mind, we return to your question. Are divination tools wrong? The answer is no. they *are only tools. The person who uses them should be open to the truth, and invite Divine guidance through them. Not restrict nor force that guidance to come through. When you use any sort of divination, don't be restricted, and listen, we might speak to you directly, and not through the tools.*

Are you aware of our guidance? Pay attention".

With this in mind, this angel cards are created. They offer guidance and support while they do not focus on future predictions. While you use them, remember to stay alert of your own higher wisdom as the angels usually speak to you directly. I encourage you to familiarize yourself with the cards and their meanings, and then, set the booklet aside and try to interpret the cards yourself. Bear in mind that one card meaning might change from situation to situation. Look at the image and the theme and connect the guidance accordingly.

TIP:

You can ask for advice for every day of the week.

<u>1. Life's purpose</u>

Indeed, you are guided towards a very successful life. You are moving fast towards expansion and completion of your life's purpose, towards your soul's desires. Don't slow down, keep moving forward. Paths will open for you, doors will appear as you walk, and people will help you achieve all that your soul desires.

We have been watching you during this life journey, and guiding you. We know all of all that which you went through up to this point and we know you are towards the end of your struggles. Your mission lies ahead of you now. If you already know what that is, then do not hesitate to walk towards it.

We are calling you from the other side of that path, nodding you to follow us, get started, and continue towards that path. You are doing wonderfully well and we are very proud of you.

As you are on this path, you expand, and so does the world alongside you. Wonderful things lie ahead at the end of that path. Don't second guess yourself. It is the right path, and it is the right time to pursue it.

If you are still uncertain about what that path is, you will find out soon. We bring you clues and guidance, so that we will help you gain clarity. Take a look around, notice all the signs: the advices from people, the repetition of ideas, places or activities. We bring it to you again and again, until you notice it. You are on the right path towards it, even if you feel lost, don't be. You are soon going to see it clearly.

Success is in the horizon and you are guided.

TIP:

It always helps sage the room before any reading. You can also light a candle and put some essential oils to help you relax and invite Divine deities in your home to help you find answers to your questions.

2. *Inner strength*

Physical or emotional pain results from the ego self. Your natural state of mind is ease and happiness. As you are struggling, as you are confused or sad, remember that these emotions are only temporary. Make the decision to let them go, as you reconnect with your true state of being.

Close your eyes for a few seconds now, with the intention of connecting with your true self. Ask that it gives you healing energy, strength and joy now. Then allow this connection to outshine any concerns and negative emotions.

You are much stronger than you think. Your higher self has so much power and joy that if you allow this connection regularly, you will feel stronger and stronger.

We believe in you and in your power. We know you can overcome any hardship and struggle. Nothing stands in the way of your powerful self. Do not be afraid, find your inner strength and walk ahead fearlessly.

3. Self-love

It has come to our attention that you are sometimes feeling incapable, lost and confused. Self-doubt makes you weak, hopeless, and alone. We are here to help you acknowledge how much you can achieve.

Don't underestimate yourself. You are powerful, unique, beautiful and very smart in our eyes. Anything you set your mind into, you can achieve.

Don't allow others to bring you down with their judgment. See with the real eyes of the source, of God, of Us. You are PERFECT.

Work passed all that makes you question yourself, so that you can move forward. This self-doubt is a blockage that keeps your for inner peace and happiness. We want to help you remove it.

Stand in front of the mirror today and speak kind words to yourself. Admire your greatness, see your beauty, appreciate your glory. You are a diamond. Find your shine and face all odds.

<u>4. Inspiration</u>

It is not time for procrastination. Your path opens in front of you now and you are invited to walk towards it. Follow through those ideas and inspiration whenever you receive it. Act! It is time to begin your great journey!

Brilliant new changes are in the horizon for you, so prepare to receive them. Do not hesitate to follow through an idea or make a change that excites you. You are on the verge for making great new changes that will be greatly beneficial to you. Listen to those ideas. Get started!

Inspiration is what will bring you expansion. Listen and act upon it.

5. *Love*

You have embarked on this physical journey

to expand and grow, love and create. Heaven sends you help, support and love. This usually comes in the form of a partner, or a person that you have a close relationship with. To receive the help from the heavens, you must open up to this person; let him/her in your life. They will help you carry on your path confident, and more fulfilled.

If you can't picture this person now, then prepare for them as they are about to join you soon. With this card, we tell you that a new romantic relationship or a new person will suffice, making your life brighter. He / she will help you mentally and spiritually grow and thrive.

We encourage you to take risks, go into gatherings and meet new people. Graciously accept assistance and suggestions that come from others as it can guide you towards this person.

If you already have this person in your life, then you are not alone. Together, your life will become a strong bond that advances you. Rely on them for support and guidance. They have the power to transform your life.

TIP:

You can also ask about past life questions and lessons.

<u>6. Review</u>

With this card, we lovingly ask you to

reconsider your current choices and state of being. You are on a path that feels uncertain, unclear, you might even feel lost. The further away you go on this path, the more lost you become. This is your state of being right now, isn't it?

You need to change your direction so that you find your peace and happiness. We ask that you reconsider your current choices. Ask yourself, whether this path fulfills you.

Don't follow choices that others make, don't ignore your intuition and happiness.

If you are uncertain, sit in silence for a while and think. What matters the most to you? What will make you happy? What changes can you do to find peace, harmony and happiness?

There are changes to be made, so make them and you will find your peace soon enough.

With this card, we encourage you to act upon your true values and happiness. We help light the way.

7. Prosperity

We see you making good investments, and purchases. As you give and receive with ease, you allow the flow of income to move from and to you.

Don't worry and obsess about finances. The universe takes care of you.

If you have worries about your income, release it. The angels want to grant your wishes for more, but your fears prevent you from acquiring them.

A big financial windfall of money will help you obtain something big that you were wishing for. Release your worries and you will receive it soon.

8. Expression

The rays of the sun find their way in, through closed doors and curtains. The way the sun shines through darkness, your life should inspire others to find their peace.

You are a mentor, a leader. You are here to make a difference in the world. You are an angel of God on earth that wraps others with their words and wisdom, and lifts them up. You spread insight, guidance and support.

In any way that you create, we encourage you to speak your truth. You have an inner connection connected with the voice of God that illuminates the souls of those who listen. Shine your light, speak your truth. You are here to inspire and make a change.

9. Manifestation

You are a great manifestator, did you know this?

Like a chief that cooks before a great meal is created, you are crafting a new project in your life that is about to come to life. As you put your energy and creativity into something, it becomes reality. Whether that is a project, a wish, a goal, we alert you that it takes form. If infused with enough energy, it becomes real to match your vibration and wish.

Keep believing in your dreams. Do not stop crafting them to life, and having faith in them. They are taking form as we speak, and they will soon manifest before your very eyes.

Well done.

10. Divine support

You are not alone at this time or any other. If

you close your eyes and pray to your guides, they will give you their guidance in different ways. As you breathe deeply and become mindful often, you will recognize their presence with you. Your spiritual team includes angels, spirits, animals and even elements such as fairies.

You were attracted to this card, because the bonding between you and them grows. Your spiritual team brings you messages and support. They want you to know that they are with you, helping you through whatever you are dealing with. Don't be afraid; just trust them to smoothen the path ahead.

A way they communicate with you is through your dreams. Before you go to sleep at night pray to them to help you find an answer. By the morning you will have clarity on what to do.

Sometimes, angels take physical form to help you through a lesson or situation. They might appear as a stranger, an animal. They usually point you to anything that will help you too, a book, a website, an idea or even a phrase.

Your guides reach out to you to let them in, to allow them to help you with this situation. They have their way on guiding you to the best idea, solution, to the perfect time, with the right people. Trust them and you will be alright. Pray and release whatever is in your mind to them now.

TIP:

You can invoke any angel, archangel or Divine Being to help you interpret the cards.

11. *Infinite supply*

Did you know that the supplies of the universe can never run out? Did you know that no wish is too big?

Don't restrain yourself, don't think that your wishes are impossible or pointless. If you wish for it, if you can think of it and feel it, you can soon experience it.

Allow yourself to recognize what you need to be fulfilled, happy and abundant. Then, simply ask for it.

Speak of it now to us. What will make you happy? What is the best resolution to the event you have asked for? What will make you feel abundant and grateful right now?

As you recognize what that is, it can be achieved in the best way and form, at the right time. The universe's infinite supplies are released with your desire. Don't restrict your needs, let them out, recognize and accept them. You are entitled to be happy.

12. *Kindness*

As you give so you shall receive. This is true not

only for material things, but for assistance as well. With this card we remind you to be open in helping others. People will ask you for help, but we will also need assistance as well.

Give without wanting anything in return.
This is the way that we help you daily, with eagerness and determination, with love and respect, so remember to do so for others.
Do not be afraid to open up to others about your needs, allow them to gift you their time and assistance, the way that you give to others, the way we give to you.
You deserve heaven's help; wherever that comes from, even if it is from people that we send in your path. Accept all the help with a smile, and remember to give it to another when the need arises.

13. *Tranquility*

Clear your schedule these days, and give time to yourself. You need rest and peace. Find some peace as it will help you relax, clear your energy, boost your positivity and find clarity on some answers you have been seeking.

You are overworking yourself. Remember that no one can benefit from you unless you are in a good condition. Put yourself first in the next few days.

As your mind finds some quiet, you can also listen to our guidance more clearly. Right now, you feel lost or confused as you need some time to recharge. Pamper yourself, treat yourself with kindness and appreciation, as you deserve it for all your hard work. Now it is time to relax and let us help you re-center.

You deserve tranquility.

<u>14. *Nurture*</u>

Mother nutriment is like no other. This card has many meanings resulting from the same theme.

The image of a loving mother holding her child has meaning that you are being taken care of.
With this card, we might want you to focus on your own mother, to remind you that she will never leave your side. Entrust her with your problems, she will give you her unconditional love.

Mother Mary's presence is dominant in this card as she is the mother of all and she lovingly takes cares of you and oversees your progress. An unexpected feeling of love and nourishment is the sign that you are in her presence.

This card also signifies the birth of a child, revealing to you that you are ready to receive what is coming next.
This is above all, a blessed card, reminding you that love is all that matters. Do not forget to take care of

yourself and give it some of that love and nourishment.

If you are a parent, your children might need you at this time. Love them, be there for them and the angels and Mother Mary will take good care of you.

TIP:

To understand what the cards tell you better, meditate before you begin your reading.

15. *Raise your vibration*

How can you enjoy what this lifetime has to give you if you disregard divine gifts? Once you look into your life you will find endless abundance of goods, people and situations that fill you with joy. Right now, you miss all of those as you focus in what does not make you happy. We ask that you shift this thinking towards your blessings instead. Notice them all around today and tomorrow. Whenever you spot something that is unpleasant, spot three more that you enjoy and love. As this becomes a pattern, your life will not be gloomy but merry and bright.

If you are wondering about a current situation, our guidance to you is to look at it from a different perspective. As you find the positive aspects of it, it will transform before you. This is the way to shift anything into a pleasant experience. Change your attitude towards it. Then, it won't be an issue or a problem any longer. You have the gift of attention, use it well.

16. *Abundance*

This card foretells goods, physical and spiritual ones. You are congratulated with gifts from the universe, with people, with happy experiences and opportunities. This card lets you know that you have nothing to worry about. You are about to be rewarded for your efforts, for your journey, for all that you are.

Heaven's gifts are showering down upon you, and they are abundant. A period of good experiences and overflow of goods is about to take place, which will last for a long time, from 2 to 6 months. At this time, you will gain new opportunities; you will be gifted with potential, with expansion, with friendships and financial prosperity. This card speaks to you about a life like the one you have been wanting; a life where you will truly be happy. Enjoy it and make it last.

<u>17.</u> *Worth*

This card reminds you of your greatness, inner and outer beauty. You have been neglecting yourself recently, perhaps even bringing yourself down. There is no greater ally than you.

Treat yourself with respect and kindness and you can conquer all challenges, and find inner peace and happiness. Let go of self-doubt and denial, you have so many talents and gifts and your inner guidance knows the right thing to do so that you prosper and thrive.

Treat yourself with dignity and love like you would do to a king. At that point, your intuition will become stronger; your confidence will help you cope with any difficulty while others will respect you even more.

We see you as radiant, beautiful and unique, and you are so loved and admired. We want to help you see just how special you really are. Do not ignore yourself, do not second guess, you are WORTHY.

If you have been procrastinating, or wondering whether you will achieve something, gain something. We tell you, don't be. Gain confidence in your capabilities and begin, you will be successful. You are capable. You can succeed in anything as long as you believe in yourself.

TIP:

To successfully read for another person, if present ask them to clear their mind and ask the angels directly the question. If the person is absent, and you know them, picture them when you shuffle the cards. If you don't know them, seeing a picture always helps to connect with their own guides.

<u>18. Release</u>

Events, circumstances, thoughts are causing you

excess stress and worry. As a result, you have been absorbing unwanted energy. As you attract this unwelcomed energy, it lowers you down. Think of a basket on the surface of the ocean. It is filled with roses and feathers, and so it is light, it floats to the surface. If you add rocks to it, it gains weight and deepens in the ocean. Similarly, if you add worry into your life, you are consumed with negative emotions and thoughts that weigh you down.

All that weight might result from your environment, from your interactions, connections or even come from your past live connections. We want to help you release all those, so that you can float easily.

If you were attracted to this card, it is time for a release.

"I ask for your assistance Archangel Michael, to help me remove any negative energy that weighs me down and any obstacles that blocks my perfect outcome/ solution to this mater. Please lift all my burdens, disconnect me from any cords that are

> *weighing me down in all depths and in all layers. I release all that no longer serves me, and I ask that you free me of them now. Thank you."*

Close your eyes and breathe deeply. Feel the energy sway and emerge through you and all around you. focus on the power that exists within you. Imagine a big sword. This is Archangel Michael's sword, he holds it now as he stands next to you. See that sword gently moving and slaying all negative cords of attachment from around you. Feel it freeing you from blockages, worry and fear. You are bound no more.

Ask him to shield you so that you don't get affected by other negative energies.

If life still feels heavy, it's because release must occur through forgiveness. Hate and resentment weighs you down. If you don't forgive you won't be able to release this weight from within you. Forgiving someone does not mean that you erase all that they have done to you; it means you release the pain they caused you.

Whatever the wrongs of another that is causing you this weight, know that it is not your place to give justice, to teach them their mistakes. Let their own life, choices and karma be the teacher. We promise you, they will finally realize the pain they caused. And so, it's time for you to lift its burden.

Write a letter to them, don't send it, just write all that you want to say to this person. Reason with them, try to place yourself in their shoes. Once this letter is completed, you've said all you needed to say, you have released whatever you felt onto paper. Pray to us to come and lift all the burdens from that letter and disconnect the pain from you, so you are free.

There are no blockages on your path at this moment, preventing you from growth, from appreciating your life and gifts.

Consider what the best outcome is, in any situation that use to worry you. As you find it, then so it shall be, there is no need to worry any longer.

19. Divine intervention

As you ask for God's divine help, know that God

hears you and sends assistance. Asking for Gods intervention does not make you weak, and it does not mean you bother us, or God. We want to help you, but you have to allow us to. Prayer is the way you do this.

As you close your eyes and concentrate, pray not with words but with emotions. This is how your prayers are understood best.

Ask for happiness and inner peace for yourself and others. As you exclude greed and selfishness, your prayers are pure and worthy of Divine help.

Allow us and God to intervene and help you now. We are ready to show you the way, to help you through this situation that will soon be resolved with divine intervention. All we ask is that you release your worry and trust that anything will be resolved. Stop overthinking the same matter, talking about it, stressing over it as that does not make you relax. All is well. We hear your prayers. Let go, and let Us and God bring you solutions.

20. *Inner peace*

With this card we let you know of resolutions that are arriving soon.

You have been worrying and obsessing about a particular matter for a while now. Dark thoughts, and unwelcomed events might be in your way now, but they are about to be lifted. A happy ending lies ahead. You don't need to worry for it any longer. Give it a few days to 2 weeks until it goes away completely.

Feel the weight lifted off your chest, as this problem persists no more.

Gain some peace of mind knowing that whatever unsettles the waters, it will cease and the waters will carry on calm and serene.

21. *Childlike innocence*

This card can bring you a few different meanings.

Find the one that identifies with you the most.

If you have children, perhaps you need to give them more of your attention and time. This is important for the children to feel loved and be able to give love as they grow. You are the most important person in our eyes, they need your guidance and support as well. Perhaps they have something to tell you but they didn't get the chance to yet. Give them the opportunity to confide in you, so that you can give them the right wisdom and guidance they need, to deal with any situation.

If you have been neglecting yourself lately, your inner child feels repressed. You need a break, a holiday, a little child-like play to unwind. Don't be so strict with yourself, take a break from all that hard work and let loose, be carefree and have some fun. Don't disregard time for you, as this is important for your being. Remember what it's like to be a kid once again.

<u>22. *Balance*</u>

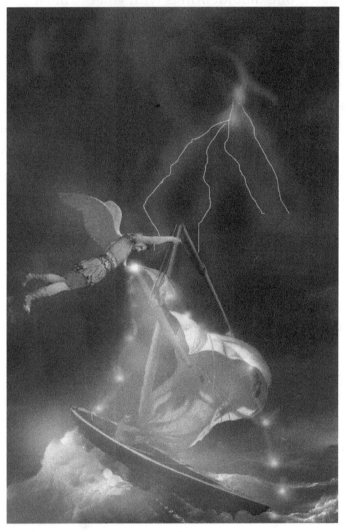

This is a period in your life where many things

happen at once, or one after the other. You might feel drained as they take a lot of your time and energy. We remind you that there is always peace after a storm.

Hang on through this turbulence; it will take you to calm waters. Remember: this too shall pass. Your life will return back to balance soon enough. Let the emotions and excess energy be washed away with the waves of the storm.

If you are considering making any changes, hold them off a bit longer. Just wait until you're certain, until the situation is more preferable.

It's alright. You are getting through this. You have our support. We see the storm passing by your home leaving you intact.

God protects you.

<u>23. Clarity</u>

An event will become clearer to you, some people's intentions will clarify, and a pathway that seemed uncertain, will finally find its purpose. Your eyes will light to the truth; you will soon realize the right thing to do.

Perhaps a situation occurred that seemed in vain, unjust, the reason for it will become clear to you.

Some people's intentions will become evident, they may hurt you in the short term, but it's better to know the truth, than hide in the shadow. If anyone worked unjustly to you, then they were not a match to your greatness. Forgive them and wish them a farewell, as their paths do not resemble your own.

Whatever you question is, with this card we light the way to the truth, so that you really see the purpose of it.

Don't worry, the truth always shines.

24. Miracle

Even if you are stressed, even if you cannot think or see a solution arising, we promise you with this card that you will soon resolve this situation with Godly assistance.

Miracles happen. Right when you are about to give up, we remind you that it's never too late. There is hope still. With this hope you will rise up strong and happy once more.

We know what you have in mind right at this moment, and we speak to you loud and clear: Don't give up, don't lose hope, keep carrying on and you will soon see a miracle in the horizon.

We are right here waving at you.

25. *past life connections*

Past life experiences give you lessons, skills and shape your gifts. With this card, we alert you that some of those gifts are yet unexplored within you. Your soul hides many talents and wisdom within. As embrace your wholeness, those become known. If you avoid spending time with yourself, loving your presence and nourishing your body and soul, then those gifts remain hidden, undiscovered. Every one of your lifetimes offered you lessons, skills and connections that last for lifetimes. This is the reason that you reincarnate so often, to gain more of those, to make your being stronger and powerful.

At this time we encourage you to rediscover those skills and listen to your inner wisdom. Perhaps what you are dealing with right now can find resolution through those skills, wisdom or past life connections. It might even originate from the past to find resolution in your present time.

To carry on from where you stand, explore your potential and talents; find your inner power to deal with any lessons that you have to go through.

Pray for a fast resolution to any karmic past life events that connect with you now. Ask for their complete release.

Explore your talents and gifts for a resolution to what you might be dealing with now.

TIP:

Don't allow anyone to touch your cards. The more you use them, the more they absorb your energy. You don't want anyone else's energy meddling with your readings.

26. *Divine timing*

People, events and circumstances need to form

to come together beautifully to co-create. At this time they are not yet ready to be seen. Have patience and be positive. Trust that the universe has a plan that works to make you happy.

Don't make any rush decisions, don't hurry into actions. Wait for us to alert you when it's time. Soon, you will understand.
God has a plan you see.

If you have questions, if you are confused, have faith that there is a plan, even if you can't understand what that is. We want you to have more faith in God, and allow the events to unfold beautifully. Within a year you will know the answer, you will know the reason. For now, simply allow the events to link one another. God is taking care of the result for you. Give your worries to God and to His Angels, to find peace.

27. Surprises

We alert you of some wonderful news. As you get this card, know that Archangel Gabriel stands behind you, excited to bring you the news.

Those might be the birth of a child in the family, the acquisition of a big gift, new property, some healing news about a miraculous recovery. Whatever that news are, they are thrilling and the angels couldn't be happier for you. You will find out soon.

28. *New talents*

You have some important tasks to attend do.

Those tasks will help to close a cycle, bring you expansion, freedom and happiness. For those to be attended to, you need to be open in learning something new.

We want to help you enrich your skills. Those skills are vital to conclude your life's mission. If you have considered in taking a new course, trying for a new job or visiting an old friend, do it. The experience will be beneficial for you.

Take actions that will expand those gifts. It's time to grow.

<u>29. *Friendships*</u>

There is no need to walk a lonely path. Open your heart to let people in.

You might have noticed that as you grow spiritually, people who do not share your energy and path tend to disappear. However, new ones are about to take their place. Allow some space for them in your life as new friendships will soon be a great part of your new life story.

You might even receive help from people close to you for something you wanted to achieve. Friends can be found in the most unlike situations.

30. Earthing

The earth calls out for you to become more connected with it. As you walk along your physical life, you forget how necessary it is to be connected with earth. You rush in your daily life, without a pause, without an earthy connection. For this, there are times that you feel disconnected, not only with the world, but within your physical body. This card is calling you to "Earth."

The good news is that earthing is very simple, but a regular repetition should be done to help you feel more at ease with yourself and your surroundings.

Stand under the sun for 10 minutes a day, spend at least half hour in your garden, surrounded by trees and flowers. Speak or pray to earth, thank it. Pause and be mindful of all that occurs with you and around you.

Fairies come very strongly in this card as well. They call for you to "let loose." Breathe and laugh. It helps to invite fairies in your garden. Every time you spend time with them, they take care of your "earthy" frequencies.

31. *Glorious awakening*

Perhaps, you spent a period recently were you felt confused.

At times, you might have felt a "haze" clouding your thoughts and judgment. Perhaps you've felt unwell psychologically, lost even.

With this card, we let you know that: no more. The fog and clouds are lifted; your path won't seem lost and aimless any longer. Your life will gain meaning, the events that take place will no longer feel pointless.

At this time, the veil of confusion is lifted; you will soon find happiness in what you do. Your life gains meaning. For some, it might even entail "spiritual awakening." Recognize your "wings" dearest one, use them to fly and be happy.

32. *Family ties*

Spend time with your loved ones. You incarnated in this life, at the same time, and in each other's lives for a reason. They have wisdom to share with you, assistance to give, so allow them to help you.

Perhaps, they need you to help them cross through a difficult path. Whatever the reason you are asked to spend time with them is, trust that it is for the highest good.

If now your attention runs through a particular person in the family, then this is the person you should reach out to the most.

If you are having a hard time, rely on your family to help you through this.

33. *Healing touch*

This card brings meaning to healing frequencies.

Perhaps you are called to explore your healing abilities. Learn to use them to help others and yourself.

If you are already a healer, then we bring attention to your gift to remind you not to let it go by unused. If you are faced with a difficulty that prevents you to use your healing as needed, then don't give up. The difficulties are about to clear away. You are called to let go of fears and trust in yourself and your God given gifts.

If you, or any of your loved ones is going through a health issue, have faith. Healing angels are surrounding you or them as we speak. Let your guard down, give your fear to God, have faith in miraculous healing. Pray and let God's work, heal.

34. *Inner connection*

Every one of you has power within. Along your gifts and talents, lies wisdom worth of many lifetimes of lessons and power. This source of power exists within and we want you to explore it.

As you find the source of connection with your inner power, your inner self, you unlock potential and guidance that comes from us directly.

The reason you have selected this card, is because you are ready to explore the Divine side of you. Find peace, to spend time with your own thoughts, to pray, so that you unlock this divine connection. The more you trust yourself, the more you meditate, and pray, the more you allow this connection to thrive and it will guide you to solve any problem with ease. This is a divine gift that you hold at heart, and you are ready to explore. It will help you understand, it will lead you towards better situations. Spend time in quiet and contemplation. Your inner power is ready to come out.

35. *Knowledge gained*

It is but Transitioning period.

The flowers and trees need time to blossom again. When their period of blossom has passed, they are in transition of new leaves and buds. Perhaps, you feel drained or sad and confused. You too need some time to recharge and gain new ideas, and will power. It is okay to feel low at times. Don't let it hold you back. Instead, allow yourself to grow strong once again and you shall rise beautiful and revitalized.

Like the cold of winter causes nature to pause its growth, your winter is worry and fear. Instead of focusing on what gives you these emotions, and trying to control an uncontrollable situation, we ask that you give it time to work out on its own. You don't need to lose any more energy and give in to fear. Rest, recharge and you will feel better. Once you do this, any situation will seem doable, will feel better. Before you take on any new tasks, take care of yourself. Let the winter pass, spring is just around the corner.

You are soon to return to ease, health and happiness. See this time as a period of learning, a period of recovery. Pause any projects, avoid people and circumstances that bring you down, and simply recharge. Know that the angels are surrounding you, helping for a smooth recovery, and returning back to joy.

Be patient, it won't be long until that too shall fade. Remember the light that shines bright within you. You have the power to go through this; don't let it bring you down.

Tip:

The messages that you receive from the cards are not only the meanings from this book, but the images or even the card numbers.

36. *Divine protection*

Other people's frequency and judgment affects you. You are vulnerable at this time. This card entails that it's time for some protection for yourself, your family, house and even belongings. The energy of others surrounds very strongly, and it drains you. Consciously or unconsciously, others pierce their own energy to you. That becomes stuck, like thorns on your aura. To request for divine protection and clarity, you create a protective shield around you, so that the thorns cannot harm you.

Protection is as important as clearing at this time, as you have already absorbed some of those "thorns" in your energy field. That might have an effect in your health, progress, relationships. Your belongings might even break down or get lost. If you have experienced any of those patterns don't disregard the signs.

Don't worry; we will guide you now into a powerful prayer for protection and clarity, so that the thorns can no longer harm you.

Clear your mind from thoughts and chatter. Get comfortable and repeat the following words:

"I ask for God's divine protection and healing for myself, my family, friends and home. I pray to you God, send me your protective angels to create a protective shield around those I mentioned, for divine protection against evil, negative entities, lower vibration of people, events, spirits or anything that tries to harm me. I ask that you surround me with your love and light at this time, to cast those away.

Let your light shine through me, through my loved ones and home, to clear away any negativity or evil deities. Let your light eliminate any effect of those that might harm, or affect me, my loved ones and my home. I am now safe, protected and cleared of all negativity in the name of the Father, the Son, and the Holy Spirit. And so it is."

Whenever you receive this card repeat this process and know that God protects you.

112

TIP:

If you receive a card that does not make sense to you, restore the whole process. Perhaps you weren't clear enough on your question, you missed a step, or you were not focused.

37. *Colorful life*

See colors all around. Slow time to appreciate the present.

The beauty that exists on earth, lies in "colors".
As you see colors all around, you see ones worth, you appreciate life, you make it more colorful, abundant, and more alive.

Make your life vibrant with colors so that you see beauty anywhere you turn, with anyone you talk to. You can beautify your own life if you don't rush from one moment to the other, if you take your time and acknowledge the beauty all around. Be mindful, speak kind words and give your attention to happy occurrences. As you do this, your life will be truly vibrant. Your purpose will be easy to reach and follow, the people that join you will be uplifting, the joy you have at heart will grow and spread through all the areas of your life that need it the most. You have the ability to make it a good happy life, start by enjoying the colors all around. In this way, you are becoming colorful yourself.

38. *Creativity*

Masterpieces and/or successful projects come to you, in order to be manifested in the physical world. At this time you are the key to such a project to come forward. You have attracted such an idea that is now in your energetic sphere, waiting to come about.

All you have to do at this time is, dedicate your time to make it happen. You will be very pleased with the results. It will bring you a positive outcome and it will be admired by others. Be the mediator that brings this project to life. It is waiting for you.

Follow your intuition and clear you mind from thoughts and chatter, and it will take form rapidly.▨

39. *Sequences*

Situations have been repeating, people have

been appearing on your path, words you have heard before are heard again. This card signifies that this cycle revolves around you very intensely, recently. Notice the patterns, hear the words, and connect with those people. Stop putting off things that need to be dealt with.

Right now, we bring you this message and hear us: these reoccurring situations need your attention. For a pattern to end, it needs to accomplish its purpose. For you to move on, to find the help you have been seeking and/ or heal and move past some situations, you need to give your attention to these patterns. They have been repeating so that you will notice, to help you move on. Stop the cycle so that you can carry on.

You might feel lost right now, not seeing what's next. This is because there are many unresolved situations that require a resolution, emotions that need clearing.

By accepting them, by not ignoring them anymore, you will finally have the chance to break free from them. Give those emotions your attention, so that they are removed. Finish projects that have been unfinished for some time. Clear your space from chatter, clear your life from any unwanted people or events.

It's time to start new.

TIP:

It's important that there are no distractions in the room when you do a card reading. This is because divine connection can achieved through intuition, and intuition can be easily heard when there is peace and quiet.

40. Bliss

We narrate this card to you with so much love

and appreciation. We want you to get a glimpse of the love we feel for you, of the love that surrounds you, of the love that is part of you, and is part of all.

We illuminate your essence in a shield of gold and white rays that resemble the sun. This is our gift to you, to receive it and experience its essence.

Stay still and close your eyes. Feel nothing else but the present. Remove any form of thoughts and just feel; experience; exist. Only two minutes is enough, but take your time with this.

We surround you at this time. We elevate you, we send you love, peace and power.

As we speak to you now, you might feel the love we give you; you might find inner peace, happiness within. This is how we want you to be, in this state. This is the state of your true essence, bliss.

You are never too far off from it. It is within reach, it lies in your quiet moments, those moments of peace, gratitude and love. In those moments when you experience any of those, you rediscover your true state of being.

With this card, we remind you of this true essence. Don't lose yourself in the ego, in the everyday problems, remember that those are only temporary, but your bliss is within you, and it exists forever.

ABOUT THE AUTHOR:

Amelia Bert is a freelance author and online journalist. At twenty five, she discovered her intuitive side, and mastered the clairaudient and clairvoyant ability to connect with spirit. She chooses to solely communicate with lighted spirits such as Angels that guide and inspire her.

She works closely with the Angels, through her psychic abilities. She gathers wisdom and information in that way, and shares it through her books and meditations. She aims to help others make a connection with their higher consciousness and discover their life's purpose.

Amelia has a degree in English language and literature. She spends her time writing, learning from the Angels, and painting. She lives with her husband and three cats and she plans to travel the world.

Find out more, visit: https://ameliabert.com

ACKNOWLEDGMENTS:

Front cover illustration:

RAZAFINDRAZAHA Mijoro Teddy, raz.teddy@gmail.com

https://www.instagram.com/mijoro.teddy/

Card illustrations:

Iqra jauhar shahzaibjouhar3@gmail.com

GET ASSISTANCE FROM THE ANGELS

Do you want to connect with Amelia and the Angels to get direct assistance on your path, and answers to your questions?

Amelia is currently offering intuitive readings with your Guardian Angels and Spirit Guides. All you have to do is reach out.

Your answers are only a few clicks away.

FIND AMELIA BERT'S BOOKS:

1. **NUMBER SEQUENCES AND THEIR MESSAGES-**

Do you get a glimpse of repetitive numbers? Do you notice number sequences like 1111, 222, 44 often? They are not random, they bring you messages. They are Angel Numbers and in this booklet, you will learn all about them. Unravel them; discover their Divine Guidance.

2. **THE GUIDEBOOK TO YOUR INNER POWER:**
This book presents spiritual practices in a step by step process to help you unleash your inner potential. Discover explanations, techniques and secrets in a broad how-to guide for all.

3. **WISDOM OF GOD, ENFOLD ME:** A team of Lighted spirits and Angels surround the creation of this book by sharing their guidance and wisdom to questions that we impose every day. Their pure Light and energy is transmitted through the words that you are about to read, bringing you the replies that you seek while inviting you towards the Light of God.

4. **THE BOOK OF DIVINE MESSAGES** - This book shares 365 divinely guided messages for daily assistance or instant support. <u>Instructions of use:</u> Clear your mind and ask what you want you need assistance with. Flip through the pages of the book and you will be guided to stop to the right message for you at that time.

5. **COLORING TO LIFE: ARCHANGES AND ASCENTED MASTERS** - This is not your usual coloring book; it is infused with spiritual power from 27 Archangels & Ascended Masters. As you color, these lighted entities surround you, sharing their energy with you for instant healing, guidance and spiritual power.

6. **THE TRUTH OF ALL THAT IS -** This spiritual book, links all the pieces together, by revealing the truth of the cosmos. Find the light and presence of the Angels beautifying your life as you right along their words. *An amazon best seller. (Also available in Spanish: "La verdad te todo lo que es")*. **AUDIOBOOK** NOW AVAILABLE.

7. **COLORING TO LIFE: DESIRES AND EMOTIONS -** This is not your usual coloring book; it provides you with 28 unique coloring sketches that present ultimate wishes and desirable emotions. As you color them, you invite their frequency to merge with your own, and ultimately manifest them into your life.

CPSIA information can be obtained
at www.ICGtesting.com
Printed in the USA
BVHW040233310820
587664BV00012B/384